WHAT DOES IT
PROFIT A MAN

Morgan D. Hill

insight *publishing group*

Tulsa, Oklahoma

WHAT DOES IT PROFIT A MAN

What Does it Profit a Man by Morgan D. Hill
Published by Insight Publishing Group
8801 S. Yale, Suite 410
Tulsa, OK 74137
918-493-1718

Unless otherwise noted, all Scripture quotations are from the King James version of the Bible.

ISBN 1-930027-63-X
Library of Congress catalog card number: 2002106948

Printed in the United States of America

CONTENTS

PART II
PUTTING IT ALL TOGETHER

Part I

The Over-Achiever

This book is divided into two main sections. The first section is an autobiographical account of my rise to become a CEO of a large corporation and the unfortunate consequences of climbing the ladder of success without God at the center of my life. The second section discusses some of the key lessons that I have learned as a result of my journey and how they can be applied to each of our lives.

CHAPTER ONE

I WAS BORN AT AN EARLY AGE

I would love to start out this book with an exciting account of my birth that somehow involves a New York taxicab during rush hour but unfortunately, there is no such account. Instead, I was born in Corpus Christi, Texas at a place called Spaun (pronounced spawn) Hospital. Although I wasn't born in a taxicab, I was born in a place named after a fish hatchery. At any rate, I was the last member to be born into a small military family—mother, father, and one older brother. My father was a fighter pilot in the Navy, so we spent the first three years of my life at the Atsugi Naval Base in Yokohama, Japan. It was in Japan that I realized that I was born with an inordinate drive and determination. It's amazing to me that as I get older, I can't remember details about yesterday but I remember this story with amazing clarity. I was barely three years of age, and I had contracted bronchitis. As a result, I had to stay at home and inside while I recovered. One day, I was home "getting better" when my family decided to go into downtown Yokohama for some shopping. I became bored and restless very quickly after everyone left. In addition, the woman that was looking after me was being mean to me—at least that was my view at the time. So I put on my coat and scarf (it was winter) and proceeded to walk out the door and attempt to find my family. This was probably the first recorded incident of a child running away "to" their parents rather than "from" them.

To give a proper perspective on this story, we lived on a military base that was on top of a large cliff that looked out over the city. The walk to downtown Yokohama was three to four miles, all heavily trafficked. I figured that I should just start walking, and so I did. I walked the entire three to four miles into the downtown area, climbed over a large wire fence, crossed a major traffic intersection, and then ended up in a shopping mall where some young American students found me. They were very nice and called the military police, which resulted in a very exciting ride home for this three-year-old adventurer. Somewhere along the way, I was less concerned now with finding my family as I was enjoying the ride with the policeman. When we arrived home, I found my family in utter panic. Needless to say, they were thrilled when I came running up the walkway. I was immediately made to lie down on the couch because I was obviously sick by my mother's diagnosis. Of course, my three-year-old logic said that I felt just great! As I reflected on this later in life, I realized that who we become is often imprinted at an early age. Although modern psychologists often attempt to label many things as having been rooted in childhood trauma or experiences, I now believe that we do become who we become based on defining events and experiences in our lives. This was truly one of those defining events.

I will not belabor a play-by-play discussion of my early childhood—because quite frankly, I am not sure it's worth talking about. Let's face it, a young boy doing chores, going to school, catching snakes, getting picked on by his older brother is fairly typical for many of us. I was raised by wonderful parents who worked to give me the best of what life had to offer. I don't believe they realized at the time that they gave me three things that would serve me well later in life—self esteem, work ethic, and faith in God. As I grew older, I have realized that self-esteem is critical to how a person approaches life's challenges. There will be some people who will always believe they are #2—the perennial runner-up in life's journey. Then there are others that believe that they can win every time. Not winning at something only toughens the resolve to win the next time. I am not advocating a win at any cost mentality, but a healthy view of yourself and abilities is essential. The second thing I received from my parents was a work ethic. As far back as I can remember all of us in the house were busy doing chores and "earning our keep." Unfortunately, like many families, my parents divorced when I was fourteen. By the time I was sixteen, my older brother and I were working one to two jobs while going to school in order to the family bills. I have no regrets at all about how things were when I was younger; however, I never really spent much time being a kid. I had to become so responsible at such an early age that I began to take life VERY SERIOUSLY. This period of time in my life was another one of those defining experiences. When you couple drive and determination with an overly serious view of the world, you get a deadly combination, an overachiever. Overachievers are an interesting breed. To the outside world, we appear to have it all. We are usually the class presidents, star athletes, honor students or all of these at the same time. I am by no means demeaning overachievers; I am one. However, I do want to point out that overachievers have the potential to have an unhealthy balance later in life. We are so driven in certain areas that we are compelled to push even harder to succeed—no matter what it takes. The third thing that I received from my parents, actually in the early years from my mother, was my faith in God. Like many people, I went to church. We went with a certain degree of regularity, but I never really understood what it was to have a personal relationship with God through His Son Jesus Christ. Because of the fervent prayers of my mother, I became a Christian at the age of fifteen. At times, I felt as though I have been connected to God with a long safety line that just wouldn't break. Even though I drifted and strained that safety line over the next twenty-five years, it never broke because of God's grace, love, and mercy.

CHAPTER TWO

I Always Wanted to Be a Cowboy When I Grew Up

I graduated from high school in 1978 as president of the student body, #3 in my graduating class of over 400, captain of the soccer team, state ranked speaker and debater all while working year round at various jobs. Remember, we overachievers look like we have the world by the tail. I graduated from high school without the slightest clue as to what to do with the rest of my life. I have always been impressed with young people who know what they want to be when they grow up. The only thing that I wanted to be when I grew up was a cowboy. First, I was born in Texas. Second, I had always dressed up as a cowboy when I was little—complete with a red cowboy hat and six shooters. So, after traveling and working for about a year and a half, I fatefully decided to go to college at Oklahoma State University—home of the Cowboys. I was careful to enroll without the red cowboy hat and six shooters. It's cute when you're five but just plain scary when you're nineteen.

I entered college thinking that I was going to be an accountant or a dentist. I chose those professions for no particular reason. In fact, I have the greatest respect for my dentist and accountant because I have absolutely no desire or real ability to look at other peoples' balance sheets or bicuspids. As I have reflected on this portion of my life, I believe that I struggled because I lacked a clear vision of my purpose in life or how I thought God would or could use me. I had become a Christian at the age of fifteen and had shown an ability to speak and teach, but I lacked the passion to enter the ministry. Deep inside my soul, I still had a restlessness that would last for many years to come. But, I had at least entered college, which would allow me a few more years to figure out what to do with my life. At least, I could say that I was a cowboy.

There is a wonderful quote from the now deceased singer and songwriter John Lennon that life is what happens to you while you're making other plans. This is perhaps the best description for how I stumbled into a career that would last for the next twenty years. I was busy working at various hospitality or restaurant jobs in order to pay my bills and college expenses. At one point, someone suggested to me that I should consider a career in this field because I was not only good at it, but I appeared to enjoy the interaction with the people as well as the pace of the business. I remember clearly telling this person that foodservice jobs were what people did who either lacked a formal education or were biding their time until a "real" job came along. Well, as fate would have it, during my second year of college, I gave in and formally enrolled in the Oklahoma State University School of Hotel and Restaurant Administration. As part of my first class assignment, I was asked to prepare a lovely dish of my own words served with a nice side salad.

I worked my way through four years of school without much fanfare. I enjoyed the hotel and restaurant industry and was taking steps to go into the hotel side of the business. I was very concerned with appearance. I figured that if I worked in the more glamorous hotel business, I could hold my head up high with my family and friends. I was quite unprepared for what was in store for me as I approached my graduation.

I have often heard it said that God looks after fools and children—probably because they need the most help. I am not sure which category I fell into, but I was in great need of God's guidance during my senior year at Oklahoma State. As is true at all universities, the senior year is the time to begin interviewing for jobs from prospective employers. I recall driving down to the local men's clothing store to buy my one and only blue suit, white shirt, and yellow tie (the clerk at the store said that this was a power color combination that was sure to impress my potential boss). I proceeded to sign up for interviews with just about everyone. Since the hotel and restaurant school had an emphasis on business administration, I talked with anyone that would interview with me—especially those companies that would fly me to their headquarters. It had become a badge of distinction if you were flown somewhere for an interview even though you may have had no intention of going to work for the company. After many months of interviewing and traveling the countryside, I finally accepted a job offer with a hotel management company based in Florida. I thought that everything was moving along just fine.

I will never forget the day that I received a phone call from a large Mexican fast food company. They were starting a brand new college recruiting program and were looking for people to interview with their company. The recruiters realized that they were starting late in the year to begin on campus interviews, but they were very eager to talk with me. Somehow, the human resource representatives had found my standard résumé (read that as college placement office mug shot) and wanted to fly me to Dallas for an interview. Even though I had accepted a position with another company, I figured that the trip to Dallas might be interesting to say the least. When I flew to Dallas, I met with an individual by the name of Frank Dyer—the Director of Human Resources. He was a sharp businessman and was very young for the position that he held. He painted this incredible picture of how a career in the fast food industry was the place for me. In fact, I met with numerous people who painted the same picture, and I bought into the complete story. After this, I knew that God looks after those of childlike faith because after this interview, I was acting like an excited child. This entire process was yet another one of those defining events for me. For the first time in my life, I was finally able to get a glimpse of what my future might hold for me. I was going to rise to the top of the corporate ladder and be a big success. I didn't realize that my climb to the top would start out with my wearing a paper hat and a polyester uniform.

CHAPTER THREE

PAPER HATS, POLYESTER, AND PIE KNIVES

The first day that I walked into my first restaurant on Clearview Parkway in Jefferson, Louisiana (a suburb of New Orleans) was a memorable one. I had just graduated from college, gotten married, and relocated to a brand new city—and it was my first day on the job. I was determined to be successful. At this juncture, something inside of me snapped. This was the point where my drive, work ethic, and goal for the future converged into a white-hot obsession. I was not going to be stopped.

I spent a total of eleven years at this Mexican fast food company and was the best of soldiers. Their culture was one of giving people challenging assignments as well as working with them to learn on the job business skills. However, the environment was often brutal on one's family and personal life. Work was all consuming. In addition to learning valuable business skills, the fast food business had a way of teaching a person about what hard work and humility was all about.

The first true experience I had that taught me about humility came when I was a new manager in training in 1983. I was working one of the many night shifts that a person is required to work as a new manager. I was told that this grueling schedule was not unlike an initiation period to see if all of the new recruits could take the pressure. Back in the early 80's, all managers were required to wear a uniform that can at best be described as disgusting. A brief description would probably be helpful. First, the manager in training wore relatively tight fitting brown polyester pants. I never understood the value of polyester except for the fact that a person could sleep in it for a week without a wrinkle. These brown pants were handsomely accompanied by a yellow short-sleeved shirt that somehow gave a yellow a bad name. Up to this point, the uniform could probably have been slightly tolerable; however, the rest of the uniform consisted of a multi-colored tie, a multi-colored vest, and multi-colored paper hat. And as bad luck would have it, the multi colors were combinations of the same brown and yellow of the pants and shirt but now with a little orange and green mixed in to just make the whole ensemble "interesting" in a freakish sort of way. On one late night shift, I was busy working behind the counter in the aforementioned outfit when I overheard the customers behind me talking about how horrible the uniform looked. Unable to curb my sarcasm, I turned and smiled at them and said that I loved my uniform so much that I actually had another one at home just like it. Needless to say, the early days of fast food taught me among to check my ego at the door because it was impossible to look suave and sophisticated in these outfits. Although I can joke about this now, I seriously believe that I learned the value of not taking myself too seriously or thinking too highly of myself. In the early days, the uniform made it impossible to get too arrogant. Later as a CEO, I found that not being afraid to get your hands dirty or wear the uniform that you expected your managers to wear while in the restaurants created an atmosphere in which people thought that you as the leader were approachable. Over the years, I have discovered that leaders connect with their followers in many ways. The more ways in which a leader can connect with others makes people want to join the organization. In addition, when a leader shows that they are human and rose through the ranks by doing the same things that the managers do, this gives people hope that they too can grow and be successful. Too often, people within an organization view the CEO as an unapproachable person who magically obtained skills that put them in a position that is unattainable to others. Leaders have a responsibility not only to provide direction for their teams, but they also must provide an environment for growth that creates opportunities for others.

The next key experience that I had in the early days taught me the valuable lesson in perseverance—doing whatever it takes to get the job done. Back in 1983 and 1984, this chain was growing restaurants at a break neck pace. I was given the opportunity to open up one of these new locations in Slidell, Louisiana, which was approximately sixty miles from my apartment in New Orleans. Being young, fearless, and full of energy, I gladly took the assignment. In addition, I said that I would happily commute the sixty miles one way each day seven days a week for the first month while we were getting the restaurant opened. I mentioned I was young and fearless-but at times not too bright. This equated to about one hundred hours per week for the first four weeks. Things went well at the opening, but I grew tired of working and commuting so much. One day I just decided to stay in the restaurant and work. I discovered that you could actually shower off your head in the wash sink and feel remarkably refreshed after thirty-six straight hours without leaving the building.

CHAPTER FOUR

LET THE LADDER CLIMBING BEGIN

This first fast food company was great at providing challenging opportunities for people without regard to age or tenure. A person received opportunities based purely on performance. I took advantage of every opportunity given to me, and I proceeded to rack up nine promotions and new assignments in eleven years. These nine positions were both corporate and field based assignments. As it relates to building a career, I found that these different jobs and experiences were very beneficial in that they gave me a varied background. Too often, an individual simply climbs straight up the ladder as opposed to making some different moves that broaden their perspective. My career could best be described as building a building instead of climbing a ladder. I held positions that oftentimes didn't result in more money, but the opportunity did allow me to work with new people and acquire new skills. There were two assignments that I took that were actually lateral moves without an increase in pay. One was in the training and development department and the other was in capital investment and planning. I didn't have formal training and experience in either of these departments. However, my superiors believed enough in me to give me a chance to broaden my skills in areas that were new and uncomfortable. Although both of these job assignments were very difficult in the beginning, the risk that I took was worth the skills that I had gained and would ultimately apply too much larger leadership roles in the future.

By the time I was thirty-four, I had been with this Mexican fast food company for eleven years. It was at this time that I set my sights on becoming president/CEO of a company. I realized that the past eleven years had given me a broad and varied foundation of experiences and business education. However, at the beginning of 1994, on my 34th birthday, I decided that it was time for me to trade what I had learned for my first major move towards becoming a CEO. I knew that the time had come for me to leave. I have to admit that the process of updating my résumé and interviewing made me feel almost unfaithful. I had eaten, breathed, and slept the culture of this company for so long, and I was a loyal and dedicated member of the team. I knew; however, that if I was going to achieve my goal, it was important for me to take risks.

The opportunity to take this risk came in a most unusual manner. I had sent my résumé out to several executive search firms. I thought that it would take me a while to get some activity, but one evening, as I was turning off the lights to my office, the phone rang. On the other end was an individual whose company had done some work for me over the years. This individual and I hadn't talked in a while. In fact, we always missed talking to each other live but were often relegated to days of telephone tag. As we were talking, he mentioned a new company that I had been reading about for several months. This new parent company had taken several well-known national fried chicken chains out of bankruptcy the previous year and were beginning to grow. On a whim, I decided to talk with them and within sixty days, I was the new National Vice President for the domestic United States. I remember feeling as though I had "arrived."

The time I spent at this new company was both a blessing and a curse. At the age of thirty-four, I was the second in command of a national restaurant chain. The positive aspects of the experience were:

- ☐ I honed my strategic and tactical business skills.
- ☐ I learned first hand leadership on a major scale.
- ☐ I learned some painful truths about the tough world of big business.

The negatives were more from the standpoint of what had happened to me on the inside. I became hungrier and hungrier for a position as a CEO. I began to push God out of my life and was determined to reach the top no matter what the cost. This hunger and ambition caused me to focus on my work like never before—to the exclusion of almost everything and everyone else in my life. I was up very early, worked very late, and traveled often. I neglected my family, my friends, my community, and my church. I was a wheel with one spoke. My situation at this time reminded me of what scientists say about frogs and boiling water. If you take a frog and throw it into boiling water, it will immediately jump out because it realizes that the water is boiling. However, if you put a frog into a pot of water at room temperature and gradually raise the temperature over time, the frog will cook. It is so unaware of its surroundings and what is happening to the water that it is too late for it to respond. At this stage of my life, I could easily have been nicknamed "Kermit the Frog" because I was in the pot with the temperature rising. I was intently focused on moving ahead—not only for myself but also for the people in the corporation. I became so hooked on the clothes, the cars, the cash, the lifestyle and attention that I would do whatever it took to rise to the pinnacle of what I viewed as success—CEO.

I spent a total of three years with this national fried chicken chain. During the end of my third year, I received a call from a group of Wall Street investors about becoming the president of one of their new investments in the restaurant business. I joined this group as the President of the holding company that owned the largest franchised bagel company in the United States. These investors had a large sum of capital backing them, and they planned to take the company public. I will always remember December 6, 1996 at my first Board of Directors meeting in Manhattan. We were on the eleventh floor of the Merrill Lynch Building overlooking Trump Tower. The Board was composed of some very powerful investors and business leaders from across the country. As I addressed them at this first meeting, I was convinced that this was the opportunity that would put me on top.

Unfortunately, my time in the bagel business was short lived. The graph of the rise and fall of the bagel business in the United States looked like the first big climb of a roller coaster —a long way up and a fast drop down. The problem with the bagel business was that it was a commodity that became a fad —a very dangerous combination. Everyone wanted a bagel, and they could get them anywhere. Unfortunately, my bagel company had no real point of differentiation from the competition. This was also true of the other bagel businesses that had flooded the market at the time. There were too many competitors with too little capital for growth to achieve a significant share of the market. As a result, the craze quickly faded, and many businesses simply ran out of money and time. Through the entire experience, I learned some beneficial business and personal lessons. On the business side of the equation, I learned a great deal about how venture capital firms operate. The bagel business was just one business out of approximately forty that this investment group was involved in. As the situation began to deteriorate, the investors stopped sending the business the cash needed to survive. There was nothing personal or emotional about the decision because it was just business. If a large ship is sinking, the captain gives the order to seal off the compartment that is leaking. The captain realizes that he has to save the ship even if that means losing the people in the flooded compartment. I quickly realized that I was not president of the ship. I was the president of a flooded compartment. During this period, I learned a tremendous amount about myself as a leader. I tested my resolve, my risk taking, as well as my determination to make things happen in spite of the obstacles. Sometimes, as a leader, you and your team just need to keep fighting regardless of the odds that are stacked against you.

Napoleon once said that leaders are dealers in hope. In order for me to truly understand this concept, I had to know what it was to experience despair. Despair is defined as not only the absence of hope but also a feeling of giving up as a result of having no hope. It was July 1997. As I mentioned previously, my bagel business venture on which I had pinned so many hopes and high expectations was coming apart at the seams. I was doing everything within my power to make the situation better, but nothing was working. In addition to my professional life, my personal life had reached rock bottom. I vividly remember walking into the living room of my home and breaking down in tears. My business and my marriage were both about to fall apart, and I didn't know how I had gotten to this place in my life. The harder that I pushed on the professional front, the worse it became on the personal front. I spent several days just going through the motions of life because I honestly believed that all that I had strived for; career, marriage, possessions were crumbling around me. It was at this point that I began some very serious soul searching. I spent several months reflecting on my life and how I had gotten so far off track. During this time, God began to help me understand five biblical and five Business Principles that would guide my life from that moment on.

Since I had lost my internal compass, God was gracious enough to enlighten me with His insights regarding directional principles for my life.

Biblical Principle #1 – Be Prayerful

**"Be careful for nothing, but in everything by prayer
and supplication with thanksgiving, let your requests
be made known unto God. And the peace of God
which passes all understanding, shall keep your
hearts and minds through Christ Jesus."
Philippians 4:6-7**

Up to this point in my life, I never really understood this concept, let alone followed it in a trusting way. God used this time of weakness and despair, to show me that if I would be prayerful, He would guide me. In addition to guiding me, He promises to give me peace on the journey. Although I don't have any children, I do have an older brother. As I think back on the traditional family vacations in our car, we constantly bugged our dad with the ever popular, "Are we there yet? Are we there yet?" I think that all of us are born with a natural curiosity for wanting to know where we are going in life and a natural impatience about getting there. I can only imagine God sometimes wanting to turn around from the driver's seat of my life and say, "Morgan, son, I love you but don't make me pull this car over." God was letting me know that it was time for me to sit in the backseat and be quiet while He took control.

Biblical Principle #2 – Be Diligent

**"Seest thou a man diligent in his business. He shall stand
before kings, he shall not stand before average men.."
Proverbs 22:29**

Many books have been written about the subject of hard work as a key to success. I have found it interesting that this is simply a biblical principle in action. The dictionary defines diligence as, "persistent in doing something . . . pursued with persevering attention . . . painstaking." As I looked at this scripture and this definition, I began to realize that the journey of life and success is often all uphill. Hiking uphill is sometimes just plain hard work. In fact, if you look at two of the words that define diligent, they are per**severe** and **pain**staking. I don't believe that it is coincidental that words like severe and pain are all part of the process. God was beginning to reveal to me that if I was going to reach my goals in life, part of the process was pain and struggling. When I was a student at Oklahoma State University, I was working my way through school at a variety of jobs at the local country club. I was attending school full time and working almost forty hours per week. One day, I was down on myself and frustrated with the entire process of school and work. I was so frustrated that I was considering giving up on a college degree entirely. I remember talking to a very wealthy businessman who owned several oil wells in the area. He began to tell me how he borrowed as much as he could from the local bank and would work for hours in the hot Oklahoma sun trying to strike oil. He said that right at the time he was about to quit drilling, he simply pushed forward a few more feet. It was at that time that he struck oil. Experts in the area told him that the place where he wanted to give up was only five feet from the oil. Ever since then, this wealthy businessman said that when times get tough and it seems hopeless, persevere and be diligent because you are probably only five feet away from success.

Biblical Principle #3 – Be Watchful

"Trust in the Lord with all thine heart and lean not unto thine own understanding. In all thy ways acknowledge Him, and He will direct thy paths."
Proverbs 3:5-6

Some people call it "luck." I have come to call it "divine intervention." This is the time when you have prepared for the battle and challenges of life and you are watchful and trusting, waiting for something to happen. And it seems that out of nowhere, something happens. Again, many people consider this luck. I like to think that if a person is prayerful and diligent in his or her pursuits, you sometimes just have to be alert for God's work to unfold. A great illustration of this principle is from the world of sports. In the 1972 Divisional Playoffs between the Oakland Raiders and the Pittsburgh Steelers, sports history records what has been termed the immaculate reception. On a 4th and 10 play with just 22 seconds left in the game, the Pittsburgh Steelers were trailing by 1 point. This final, last-ditch play was a pass. The ball was deflected from its original receiver, and fullback, Franco Harris, who wasn't even supposed to be "in" the play scoops the ball up just inches from the ground. He not only grabs the ball inches from the ground, but he runs 42 yards for the winning touchdown giving the Steelers a 13-7 victory over the Raiders. The coach for the

Pittsburgh Steelers gave the following quote about this remarkable play: **"He [Franco Harris] was hustling and good things happen to people who hustle."**

It would have been so easy for Franco Harris, the fullback, to have just gone through the motions for this final play. It was a pass play, and he was a running back. He shouldn't have been anywhere around. But as his coach said, he was hustling and good things happen to people who hustle. I believe that there is a clear biblical principle at work as well. Sometimes, we simply need to be working, hustling, and trusting that God is going to make a big play happen. We need to be watchful for when God begins to move in our life or we will miss out on great opportunities. And sometimes, those opportunities come disguised as problems or plays that didn't go exactly as planned.

Biblical Principle #4 – Be Thankful

"Bless the Lord, O my soul, and forget not all His Benefits: Who forgiveth all thine iniquities, who healeth all thy diseases, who redeemeth thy life from destruction; who crowneth thee with loving kindness and tender mercies; who satisfies thy mouth with good things so that thy youth is renewed like the eagles."
Psalms 103:2-5

I am constantly amazed that as I get older, I can remember specifics from my childhood with great clarity. One of the lessons of my childhood that has stuck with me throughout my adult life is the concept of "magic words." When I was growing up, if there was ever a time in which I was demanding something of someone, usually my parents, they would say, "What's the magic word?" Invariably, it was one of two, "please" and "thank you." Please and thank you began to form a foundation not only of just good manners, but also I found that these two words oftentimes had mystical powers. If I simply said one or both of these words, I could get "stuff." If I ever said them as part of a sentence beginning with "please" and ending with "thank you", I thought that the whole world was my mine for the taking. After looking at life as well as looking through the Bible, I have come to believe that an attitude of thankfulness is not just good manners but it brings abundance beyond our wildest imaginations. Matthew Chapter 14 chronicles one of the accounts of Jesus feeding the multitudes with a few loaves and a few fish from a small boy's lunch. I have often listened to Bible critics who have tried to explain that this was not a miracle but rather just a great job of portion control. In the 19th verse, Jesus blesses the loaves and the fish and gives thanks to God for what they have before them. The writer Matthew explains that not only were thousands fed, but they were full, and there was food to spare (twelve baskets full to be exact). I believe that this miracle resulted from a mixture of <u>faith and thankfulness</u> and it produced an abundant miracle in which God was glorified.

I had grossly forgotten this concept in my life, and even today, I find it so easy to take all that we have for granted. I have begun to relearn this principle that was very sound for me as a child. Say please and thank you for all that we get in life and God will work miracles not only for us but for those around us.

Biblical Principle #5 – Be Confident

"David said, 'The Lord that delivered me out of the paw the
lion and the paw of the bear, He will deliver me out of the
hand of this Philistine.' Then David said to the Philistine,
'Thou comest to me with a sword, and with a spear, and a
shield; but, I come to thee in the name of the Lord of Hosts,
the God of the armies of Israel, whom thou has defied.'"
1 Samuel 17:37,45

As I have studied the Bible over the years, I am truly
amazed at the story of the life of David, especially the account
of him as a youth. In this story, David was nothing but a young
shepherd boy on an errand for his father. He stumbles into a
situation that he couldn't believe. The Philistine army and its
leader, Goliath, was openly defying God and His army, and
David was stunned to see that no one was doing anything
about it. The story talks about how David tried to go out into
battle with all of the traditional armor of war, but it didn't fit
him figuratively or literally. So instead, he decided to go out
and battle the way he knew best—with a sling and a stone.
There are several key points to highlight from this story and
how it relates to David's confidence in God:

David had seen God's power before – The scripture above says
that David knew firsthand that God could work in mighty and
mysterious ways because He had helped David slay a lion and
a bear while tending his father's flocks.

David knew the power of positive words – The Bible has spoken for years what modern authors have mentioned about the power of a positive confession and affirmation. There is true power when a person combines fervent belief with positive words. Proverbs 18:21 says that death and life are in the power of the tongue.

David backed what he had seen and said with action – It would have been one thing for David to have seen God's hand in his life and to make a positive confession on the battlefield, but he backed up those two things with action knowing that God was with him.

David played to his strengths and did what he knew best – Instead of giving in to conventional thinking and wearing the battle armor of the day, David had to fight the battle with Goliath with the tools that he knew best—a sling and a stone. Too often, people do not use the God-given strengths and talents that are right in front of them to confront life's challenges. When we move ahead to attack the giants in our life, we do it from a position of weakness, which can be disastrous. The great management guru Peter Drucker was once quoted as saying that leaders should spend more time becoming great at what they're good at rather than trying to become good at what they are bad at. As the old boxing saying goes, "Don't lead with your chin, you'll get knocked out every time."

I believe that true confidence is based on a building block process in which one stage builds upon another so that one's actions are really the tip of the proverbial iceberg. When I was growing up, my brother and I used to build forts. I am not sure if kids today still build forts, but we did, a lot. We started with simple forts that we built in our bedrooms. These forts were very shaky at best. They were usually comprised of an intricate and delicately placed network of books and lamps holding blankets and sheets over furniture. There were many times in which our forts came crashing down around us with the slightest movement. As we grew a little older, we graduated to building tree forts. My brother and I thought that it would be a good thing for us to take our questionable building skills and go up into a tree. There was more than one occasion in which we gingerly stepped out onto our woodland fortress, only to have the whole thing come tumbling down around us. I will never forget when I was about seven years old and my brother was around ten, that our father built a real fort for us in the backyard. I will always remember that first time climbing onto that fort and jumping up and down on it. I was truly amazed that it withstood all of our boisterous behavior. Nothing that our seven and ten year old minds could devise could even shake or rattle that fort.

As I began to look at these five biblical principles, I started to see that they were like building blocks that built upon each other to the point where you could stand at the top with confidence and not shake or rattle its foundation.

<u>Building Block 1</u> – *Be prayerful* – This is the true foundation for guidance in our life. We must realize that God has a plan for our life and we must commit that to God through our prayers. We must then rest in the knowledge that God is driving the car, not us.

Building Block 2 – *Be diligent* – There is nothing more important in our life than committing ourselves to hard work and determination in spite of the obstacles. We must get moving forward in the direction that God is leading us. Someone once told me that you can only steer a ship that is moving. There may be times that you need some course correction. God can work with each of us if we are prayerful and working to make things happen.

Building Block 3 – *Be watchful* – When prayer and preparation meet the unexpected opportunity, great things can happen. Most often, these unexpected opportunities come out of left field and are disguised as headaches that no one else would touch with a ten foot pole. The great statue of *David* carved by Michelangelo was made out of a forty year old piece of old, misshapen, and discarded rock. Yet, out of this piece of rubble, Michelangelo carved perhaps the greatest masterpiece that the world has ever seen.

Building Block 4 – *Be thankful* – I have come to believe that an outward spirit of joy and thankfulness is a key to a happy life. Enjoying the journey is the most important aspect of life and not waiting until some point in the future to be happy and thankful for God's blessings in each of our lives.

Building Block 5 – *Be confident* – Once we have begun to stand on these first four principles, we can approach life's challenges with a divinely inspired confidence. We can jump around on our fort and know that it is sturdy and secure.

It took several months for these lessons to sink in. Although I was glad that God was showing me these insights, I was still in trouble. My career was about to go up in flames, so I decided to step out in faith and begin rebuilding my fort. I prayed that God would help me out of what seemed to be an impossible situation in my bagel business. In addition to prayer, I not only tried to revive my business, but I looked at starting other business opportunities with my investors. I remember walking around our tiny little office in Atlanta and telling my staff that something great was going to happen. I knew these principles were sound, and I refused to give up. One day, a gentleman that worked with me came into my office and sat down. He knew that business was tough, and that I was doing all that I could to make the business flourish. He said that what I needed to do was to network more with other business leaders in the Atlanta area. At the time, we were struggling to meet all of our expenses; I couldn't manage to buy myself lunch, let alone network and power lunch with other successful businessmen in Atlanta. But, on a whim, I decided to call a very successful businessman in the Atlanta area. He was the founder and chairman of a large multi-million dollar restaurant company. In fact, he owned several chains. I thought to myself that all that could happen is that this person would laugh at me or simply not return my phone call. I remember placing a phone call on a Monday morning at around 9 A.M. By 10 A.M.. I had received a phone call. Within four weeks, I had negotiated to sell my bagel business back to my investors, and I had become the new President of two fast-food chains with annual sales of $250 million. In addition, I was able to transfer the members of my office staff to the new company. God did the unexpected and great things happened when disaster was almost a certainty.

CHAPTER FIVE

BE CAREFUL WHAT YOU WISH FOR.
YOU JUST MIGHT GET IT.

There is an old saying, "Be careful what you wish for or you just might get it." I think that is the best way to describe my getting promoted to president and later CEO. I had wanted to get to this place my entire career, and now I had arrived. Unfortunately, there were still some hard lessons that God would have to teach me over the next several years.

I began my new assignment as president of these two chains with great vigor and enthusiasm. The businesses were in a real mess, and for some strange reason, I just loved it that way. To give a bit of background information, these two regional fast food chicken chains compete in the eastern United States. They had each been around for many years and had their share of wins and losses in the game of business. There were about 350 restaurants around the country owned by both the franchisor as well as franchisees. The two chains were now currently owned by another large fast food company who had struggled with exactly how to grow them since they specialized in another area of fast food. This parent company simply ushered me in and gave me full freedom to do whatever I thought was best to turn things around.

Whenever I approach a new challenge, I have a certain creative process that I go through. I work to focus on both the immediate and the not so urgent. It is what I have come to call **bi-focal leadership**. I believe that a leader needs to develop the ability to work not only on the urgent issues, but also on the long term ones. They must engineer solutions with a team of people that create opportunities for everyone. So in my office, I would pour over countless documents and research information—everything that I could get my hands on. In addition, I took out all of the nice furniture that had been given to me and put in flip charts and dry erase boards. I had notes and pieces of paper taped all over my office. I know that other people in the office were a little alarmed that my office seemed to be a disaster area of paper and notes. It was the equivalent of driving through a very nice neighborhood, only to see one of the neighbors with an old beaten up car in the driveway that was a "fixer upper." I assured everyone that this creative thunderstorm would produce some long overdue rain for these two restaurant chains. I worked late into the night on this paperwork, and during the day I was busy as president out among the troops as well as spending time in the restaurants learning how the business operated.

After about ninety days of doing this, I laid out a very simple plan that involved two key points:

1) **Improve our financials, pay our bills, or go out of business**
2) **Develop a long range plan to grow**

I know that seems incredibly obvious, but we were in such financial difficulty that we were not paying all of our bills. The bills were being paid by our parent company. There were all sorts of reasons for this, but the fact remained, that we were not carrying our own weight and that was unacceptable. So I set about the task of rallying everyone around the cause and creating a sense of urgency that something needed to be done to fix the problem. We brought everyone together and shared the current reality of our problem. During this time I began to learn how difficult leadership can be when you are trying to move people in a new direction. When you start out, many times only the leader has a vision of the future, yet you have a responsibility to bring your people with you. I can only imagine what Moses must have felt like as he had several million Jews out in the desert after leaving Egypt. He was virtually a "one-man show" trying to lead everyone to a new and better promised land. The bible speaks about how Moses' father-in-law, Jethro, provided extremely wise insight. He advised Moses to develop a team of leaders who work with him to guide the children of Israel into the Promised Land. Shortly after I laid out the short term plans to turn around the company and was met with the natural onslaught of issues and complaints, I quickly discovered my own Jethro in my administrative assistant. One especially frustrating day, I remember that she came up to me and said, "No matter how right you may be, if the rest of the people don't follow you, you will fail like everyone before you." That wisdom of her words stopped me dead in my tracks. It was at that time that I began to develop my team of direct reports who would help make things happen. The great philosopher Lao Tzu put it best in the Tao Te Ching when he said, **"With the best of leaders, when the work is done and the project is complete, the people will say that we did it ourselves."**

In January of 1998, my team and I set about the task of turning around these two regional chains. In the early days, it was like a fire brigade. I was able to assemble a team of cross-functional experts whose task it was to help me "fix" the immediate problem. And fix the problem we did. I always find it amazing that when you get people together around a crisis, great things begin to happen. We started to experience our first successes and people were beginning to feel that they could win after they had almost forgotten what it felt like. While we were all working on the problems at hand, I also began working on the long-range plan and vision for the company. This was both an exciting and frightening process. As the leader, you have a responsibility to point to the future as an exciting place for others to follow but at the same time include them in the process. I will never forget how everything began to come together as if divinely inspired. It was March 2, 1998, and I was returning to Atlanta from a quick business trip to Los Angeles. I had decided to take the late night flight back so that I wouldn't lose a day of work. I had been working on the plans for the future while at the same time working with the team on the pressing issues of company profitability. I remember sitting at the back of the plane at around 2:30 A.M. when it suddenly hit me—the vision for the future of the company. I began to scribble wildly on a piece of yellow legal paper, and within 1 hour, I had crafted the crude outline for a new plan for growth for the organization.

I came back to Atlanta with an excitement that I just couldn't contain. As I shared my visions of the company with my team, they were very receptive. In essence, we would develop a new parent company that would spin off from the existing parent company. This new parent company would acquire the two existing chains as well as other chains for future growth. Everyone was excited, but we had no idea how we would accomplish this task.

Over the next several months, the team and I worked feverishly on a business plan for the future growth of the company. It would not only provide opportunities for people to grow but also would inspire people in the organization. During this time, the team and I stumbled on to five Business Principles that we believed were crucial to helping an organization and its people reach their full potential.

Business Principle #1 – Dream Big Dreams

"Believing in the unlimited potential that lies within all people and are being committed to providing opportunities for people to achieve their dreams."

There is a great quote by Bernard Edmonds that says, "To dream anything that you want to dream, that is the beauty of the human mind. To do anything that you want to do, that is the strength of the human will. To trust yourself to test your limits, that is the courage to succeed." A lot has been written in modern business literature about this subject. As I observe the landscape of great accomplishments, it all began with a dream that others would often think is foolish or unrealistic or sometimes dangerous and life threatening. I remember driving along a road in Tampa, Florida a number of years ago on a business trip. I passed by a church on July 3rd that had on the marquee for the Sunday sermon, "What if the Founding Fathers had lost the Revolutionary War?" Up until that point, I don't know that I had ever really given that question any serious thought or quite frankly if I had ever really thought about that question at all. As a young boy growing up, I studied my history books just like everyone else. I assumed that we would win the war, versus looking at it as a risky venture that could have failed. I just finished a wonderful book that chronicles the events of the Revolutionary War and the leaders who had the courage to dream big and risk everything for what they believed. I recently celebrated my 42nd birthday, and I realized that many of the Founding Fathers were around my age when they started fighting for their independence from Great Britain. The chronicles of the war showed that the colonies never should have won the war because all of the odds and sound logic were against them. This is why dreaming big is so important because it lifts everyone above and beyond themselves and aligns them toward something of greater importance. This is often how extraordinary results are achieved through ordinary people who are inspired and dare to dream.

Business Principle #2 – Play Your Best Everyday

**"I can't imagine a person becoming a success who doesn't give this game of life everything he's got."
Walter Cronkite**

I have often struggled to find the balance in this world between "playing your best" and winning at all costs. I believe that we exist in a culture of scorekeeping. From our most tender years, we are placed in competitions and comparisons to those around us. Perhaps my parents did this when I was growing up, but it seems that today, more and more parents are taking note of who rolled over first, who stood up first, who formed sentences first and who was potty trained first. I have no recollection of when I did any of those things. I believe that my parents were probably thrilled when I stopped eating dirt out in the yard. However, at some point, all of us cross this threshold of competition that encourages and rewards winners and disdains losers. As we get older, the score is: the house you live in, the cars that you drive, the vacations you take, etc. I don't think that there is anything inherently wrong with enjoying the fruits of your labor and there is nothing wrong with striving to be the best that you can be in life. However, we rarely reward or applaud the effort, only the end result. When I was growing up in Virginia Beach, Virginia, I had a friend named Ben Trotter. Ben was and I'm sure still is a great guy. He was tall and athletic and everyone liked him. I remember that in junior high, he was a star athlete, but he did not make the best grades. I recall talking with Ben about a test in which I barely studied and got an "A" and Ben studied his heart out and got a "C." Ben used to take the best notes and would even stay after school with the teacher to go over the material to be sure that he really learned it. I learned a lot about the principle of playing your best from Ben Trotter. He gave 100 percent and never gave up the fight. His best grade was only a "C," and I admired him for never quitting.

The 1999 Super Bowl between the St. Louis Rams and the Tennessee Titans is perhaps the finest example of "Playing Your Best" that I have seen in recent memory. Over the last ten years or so, I had all but given up on Super Bowls. Somehow, they just deteriorated into a lopsided football game with an over-produced half-time show stuck in the middle. Anyway, my neighbor invited me over for this Super Bowl, so I finally decided to go, mainly because my neighbors are great people, great cooks, and I knew that there would be some tasty snacks. As it turned out, this game was a literal clash of the titans from the opening kickoff. The score teetered back and forth throughout the entire match. On the final play of the game, the Titans were behind and they needed a touchdown to win. On an amazing play, Titan receiver Kevin Dyson broke free with the ball and was headed for the game-winning touchdown. In a last ditch effort, Rams linebacker caught up with Dyson and grabbed his legs so that Kevin couldn't move. As Kevin was just a few feet from the goal line and Super Bowl victory, he made one last effort to score as he was falling to the ground. He thrust his arm out with the ball toward the goal. He missed the touchdown by inches. The gun sounded and the game was over. The Rams won and the Titans lost, at least that was what the scoreboard said. But there wasn't a football fan anywhere that didn't stand and cheer Kevin Dyson for his valiant effort. He played his best even up until the end and never gave up.

Business Principle #3 – Build Trust With Others

I have come to the conclusion that three-year-olds are perhaps the most fearless and trusting creatures on the earth. I have reached this conclusion after spending countless hours at the neighborhood pool. As a kid growing up, I was in the water more than most fish. I loved going to the pool. I will never forget piling what seemed to be a hundred kids in a four-passenger car (trunks were larger in the early days) and zooming off to the local pool. Of course, the pool had the segregation process— boys on the right, girls on the left. We had to go through the locker room so we could make all of the final preparations. It was essential to get all of our aquatic gear in order for the various games and water warfare that would take place. We would leave the locker room with gear strapped on and then pass through the pool showers. To this day, I never really understood the purpose of the showers— why get wet <u>before</u> jumping in the water. At any rate, I learned how to swim when I was just three years old. I learned by simply jumping in and thrashing about wildly. I remember my parents in the water gently urging me to jump in. I needed little urging because I simply got a running start and leaped from the side of the pool into the arms of my parents. I was absolutely fearless as were all of the other three year olds at the pool. Having mastered swimming quickly, I decided to venture to the high diving board. It was probably only about twelve to fifteen feet high, but to a child, it was like scaling the Empire State Building. I remember standing at the edge of the board and looking over the sea of bathing suits trying to find my mother. It was important for her to watch EVERYTHING that I did because that's what I thought mothers wanted to do. With an encouraging "Go ahead and jump sweetheart" from my mother, I ran off then end of the board squealing all the way into the water. I loved it! No fear, no hesitancy, and no wondering if my mother was giving me bad advice. It was just pure fun and excitement.

Sometime after that, things begin to change. Perhaps it's the first time your friends or perhaps an older sibling encourages you to do something. After you step out in good faith, you realize they have taken advantage of you. I do believe that is why young kids run to their parents. They are the people that they know they can trust. As I have gotten older, I have learned that trust is really the glue that holds everything together. Before anyone can trust another individual, that person must be individually trustworthy. Trustworthiness both personally and professionally are the combination of two factors—character and competence. Character can be broken down into three subsections:

1) Integrity – being true to one's values, feelings or commitments
2) Maturity – expressing yourself with courage and consideration
3) Abundance Mentality – believing that there is enough for everyone.

When I was younger, my brother, father, and I spent time camping in Maine. I will never forget the first time my dad showed me how a compass works. As we were hiking and canoeing, he would take his compass out, and it would always point "North." Not sometimes or when the weather was good or the winds were blowing just right but ALL OF THE TIME. One's character has often been described as a person's true north. No matter what the circumstances, a person's integrity, maturity, and abundance mentality will always point north. Others learn that they can count on them each and every time.

The other part of trustworthiness that is equally important is the concept of competence. Like character, competence is made up of three things:

1) Technical competence – one's practical knowledge and skill related to one's field of expertise
2) Conceptual competence – knowledge and skills such as planning, forecasting, insight, problem solving, etc.
3) Interdependence – the ability to work with others

My dad was a jet fighter pilot in the Navy for many years. He learned how to use a compass and navigate by using the stars and other landmarks at an early age. When we went camping and he would take out his compass, he would not only show me that it was pointing due north. He would also teach me how to use the compass technically so that I could find out where we were if we were lost. The compass would have been far less useful to us if my dad didn't know how to use it correctly to solve our problem. I always felt safe and secure knowing that my dad knew how to use the compass (competence), and he always knew where "north" was located (character). When we were in the woods, my dad was trustworthiness personified.

I have spent more that half of my life so far in the business world. There, I learned some very valuable lessons about trust. As I said, I believe that trust is the glue that holds everything together. Unfortunately, the business world is full of people who may not have the internal compass that points "True North." Instead, the needle points back to them and they seem more concerned with what is in it for them versus how to help out someone else. This is the cause of all sorts of battles and political agendas. In my early days, I just couldn't believe that everyone didn't abide by the same set of values and principles that I did. It was so easy in those days to become jaded and disillusioned. Many people unfortunately abandon their own internal compass for direction and begin to play the game of business by a new set of rules; <u>Everyone looks out for himself or herself</u>. Although this may generate short-term results or even get people the monetary reward that they desire, it is not the credo by which to live your life or to be known by others. At one of the companies I worked with recently, I came across a great model for creating trust between others once you have established your own sense of individual trustworthiness. The acronym is as follows:

Truthfulness – always tell the truth. Not just not lying, but a willingness to set out and tell it like it is no matter what.

Results – get the job done. People are looking to you to make things happen

Understanding Motives – others must believe that your interests are to promote the welfare of everyone and not just yourself

Skill – always improve your skill and knowledge. Lifelong learning

Team Player – with great leaders, when the job is done the people will say we did the work ourselves. Always promote the welfare of the team

Leaders in today's business world provide guidance and direction to the people in their organizations. In addition, perhaps the greatest need that people in an organization have is that they can trust their leaders to do the right thing. Leaders must make decisions with the best interests of the organization in mind. More than ever, leaders need to be reminded to check their own internal compass to be sure that they are guiding those following them to the right destination.

Business Principle #4 – Enjoy Yourself Along the Way

"A merry heart doeth good like a medicine"
Proverbs 17:22

If laughter is the best medicine, then I have become a twenty-four-hour a day pharmacy. I don't know what happened, but somewhere along the way, I developed a sense of humor. On balance, I have come to believe that most of what we get worked up about, really isn't worth getting worked up about at all.

As I was growing up, I always enjoyed a good joke but I remember very clearly always being the serious one. One of my good friends growing up was a boy named Randy White. Randy was the funniest kid in grade school. He was constantly doing things that made all of us laugh and usually got himself in trouble while doing it. I was a little bit envious of Randy's natural ability to make an entire room full of fourth graders laugh. Back then I thought the class clown was king! Given that my brother and I were the main breadwinners in our family at an early age, everything seemed to get pretty important pretty quickly. There was no playing around. I recall being in school plays being cast in the more "adult" roles. Whenever I would give speeches, I would always be perfectly rehearsed with no humor. Well, that mind set and approach to life seemed to follow me until I was about twenty-five years old.

When I was twenty-five, I was working for the large Mexican fast food chain I mentioned earlier. I was a training instructor in Atlanta, Georgia. I was so excited to get this job because I loved public speaking. I was part of a four-person office team that would do classroom and field based instruction for the Southeastern United States. We would normally give presentations on everything from management motivation to how to shred cheese. Well, as fate would have it, I was paired with another instructor who was the equivalent of Randy White. My ultimate dream job had turned into a nightmare. This other instructor, Jonathan Lindley, was very funny. I will never forget those first few months listening as an entire classroom of students would roar with laughter as Jonathan was teaching. When I began to teach, however, the laughter would stop. At the end of every week, the class would give each of us written evaluations on our performance. The long and short of hundreds of evaluations was, "WE LOVE JONATHAN!" Morgan is a bit too serious." One fateful Saturday afternoon, after one of our classes had just graduated, I was called in to the manager's office to discuss my evaluations. I was devastated when he told me that I was not performing up to standard and that I needed to improve. I was hurt and indignant. I began to justify how my teaching was thorough and insightful versus overly playful. Then my manager gave me some wise advice, "If people don't connect with you, they won't listen to you." I left that meeting without the slightest clue as to how to fix my problem. How does a person become funny?

For the next several weeks, while we didn't have any classes in session, I racked my brain as to how I was going to lighten up, be funny, and still get my point across. I will always remember the day that I cracked the code. It was late afternoon and I was teaching a class on customer service to about sixty-five managerial students. I began to tell a story in which I was absolutely ruining the best restaurant due to my poor management skills. The classroom was roaring as I shared a common experience in which I blew it. It was a that moment that I learned a few key lessons about humor, business, and leadership:

☐ People like to know that leaders make mistakes.
☐ Laughter gets people to open up and connect like nothing else.
☐ You can laugh, have fun, and still get the work done.
☐ It's okay to laugh at yourself.

Later on as I grew up in business, I worked diligently to maintain a balance between being serious and having fun. Some companies say they want you to enjoy yourself at work, but scold employees when they do. As I became a CEO, I encouraged people to laugh. In addition to being stress relieving, laughter also stimulates the creative centers of the brain. I had a very simple rule of thumb, "If people aren't laughing, then they aren't enjoying themselves." It was amazing that people could work and have fun all at the same time. There are some great words of wisdom from a Kentucky woman named Nadine Starr. A few of her words of wisdom goes something like this:

If I had to live my life over . . .

☐ *I would like to make more mistakes next time . . .*
☐ *I would relax.*
☐ *I would be sillier than I've been on this trip.*
☐ *I would have taken fewer things seriously.*
☐ *I would take more chances.*
☐ *I would eat more ice cream and less beans.*
☐ *I would perhaps have more actual troubles, but . . .*
☐ *I would have fewer imaginary ones. . . .*

Business Principle #5 – Make an Impact on the World Around You

**"It is truly amazing what can be
accomplished when no one cares who gets the credit."
Robert Woodruff—Coca Cola.**

When I was thirteen years old, I was living in Virginia Beach, Virginia. As I recall, thirteen is a bad age because you seem to be stuck in the neutral gear of life. You are too "old" to be with all of the little kids in the neighborhood, but you don't seem to be old enough for the exciting stuff like driving a car or getting a real job that would give you a paycheck every two weeks. So the summer that I was thirteen, I resigned myself to this cruel twist of adolescent torture and decided to take on odd jobs around the neighborhood to earn money. I will never forget that one of the jobs that I got that summer was from my dad. He wanted to put in a garden in our backyard. Based on his knowledge of horticulture, this required the largest truckload of topsoil that anyone could imagine. This mound of dirt was GIGANTIC! My father said, "Morgan, I will pay you $27 if you move this topsoil from the driveway into the backyard." I love my dad a lot, but of course, his offer of $27 for me to move this dirt was kind of like Marlon Brando in the movie *The Godfather* making an offer that you just didn't refuse. I remember saying "yes" to my dad's job offer and then going outside to look at this huge pile of dirt. I couldn't imagine that I was ever going to do it.

Well, a few days went by after my father made the offer. I would walk all around the mound of dirt , thinking that somehow my staring at it would either make it move on its own or miraculously get smaller. I finally decided that this initial approach was not getting me anywhere, so I got out the shovel and wheelbarrow and began the monumental task. It seemed as if I worked for days and didn't make the slightest dent in this Mt. Everest of topsoil. I had been at it for several days when my dad came by and said, "Morgan, it really looks good, you are making progress." Slumped over the shovel like a third leg and covered from head to toe with sweat and dirt, I looked up at my dad with a look that only thirteen year olds have learned to perfect. It's a mixture of disgust and exhaustion all rolled into one. I didn't dare say anything to my dad other than, "Thanks."

Eventually, I finished moving all of the topsoil, and my father and I proceeded to plant row after row of vegetables. I remember that first night when my dad and I picked some of the fresh vegetables that we had grown and brought them into the house for dinner. They tasted like nothing that you would buy at the store. Somehow, at that moment, the seemingly impossible task wasn't so impossible and the tasty rewards for me and my family were worth it.

As I reflect on that story, I learned some valuable lessons about "making an impact" that served me well later in life.

- ☐ **When there is a big job to get done, procrastination doesn't make it smaller.**
- ☐ **If you are going to make an impact on something, it often happens one shovel-full at a time.**

☐ When you are in the middle of something big, you often
    don't notice the difference you are making unless someone
    points it out to you.
☐ When you begin to taste the fruits of your labor, all of the
    hard work seems to be worth it.

Even though I was only thirteen at the time, I believe that the
lesson that I learned stayed with me for years to come and
helped shape my view of this 5th business principle or perhaps
more appropriately labeled life principle. Much has been
written over the years about the topic of making an impact—
making a difference in the lives of others and the world
around you. It seems that most everyone goes through a
process in which they work to find some sense of meaning to
their life other than the day to day hustle and bustle of activity after activity. One of the most insightful books written on
this topic was by Dr. Viktor Frankl in *Man's Search for
Meaning*. In this book, he recounts the horrors that he and
countless others suffered while imprisoned in the concentra-
tion camps of Nazi Germany. Out of this experience, he developed a revolutionary psychotherapy called Logotherapy. At the
core of his theory, Dr. Frankl believes that a person's primary
motivational force is his or her search for meaning in life. We
all want to know that we have made a difference in the lives of
others or in the world around us.

I personally struggled with this concept for many
years. As I was on my path to become "CEO of the Universe,"
I was content for a time to simply drop my check in the col-

lection plate at Christmas or Easter or perhaps to give a few dollars to the United Way. I looked at the issues that surrounded me, and I believed like most people believe that someone else would grab the shovel and move this huge mound of dirt. Even as I behaved this way on the outside, I continued to struggle on the inside with a desire to do something that made a difference with my life, but I had no idea where or how to start. This struggle came to an emotional climax in 1997 while I was on a trip to India and Nepal.

I had taken a train to Agra, India to see the Taj Mahal. It was truly a spectacular site. I was enjoying sight-seeing with my guide until it was time to be dropped off at the train station for the ride back to New Delhi. During the day, I had a chance to see sights of incredible beauty and incredible ugliness. My comments are not meant to insult anyone from India. This situation could have played out anywhere in the world. But as I sat at the train station, I watched for two hours as children with deformed legs crawled along the platform begging for food. I watched as people fought and argued with each other. I listened to this foreign businessman tell a group of Indians how worthless and horrible they were and how they deserved the conditions that they lived in. The more I listened, the more overwhelmed I became. I had no idea what I could do or how I could help. I was wishing that it would go away, but the reality kept hitting me in the face and in the heart, over and over and over. I began to cry on that bench at the train station in Agra, India. The lesson that I learned when I was thirteen came flooding back into my mind and soul. You can make an impact on the lives of others and the world around you, one shovel full at a time. Instead of trying to change the whole world, I decided at that moment to begin the process of changing the world around me, however large or small that might be.

When I got back to the states, I began to think about Jesus and His impact on the world. He didn't have mass media at His disposal. He didn't possess great earthly wealth. He didn't command an army. He didn't travel all over the world to preach His message of redemption. He spent most of His time pouring His life into the lives of twelve men who would ultimately change the world. Making an impact and making your life mean something often happens with the people closest to you right in your own backyard.

There's the story of a little boy who was walking up and down a very large beach that was filled with starfish that had washed ashore during a storm. The little boy was painstakingly picking up each starfish and throwing them back into the water so that they wouldn't die. An older gentleman came up to the boy and asked what he was doing since there were hundreds and hundreds of starfish. The little boy replied that he was trying to save all of them so that they wouldn't die. The old man said that the boy was being foolish. Since there were so many, it just didn't matter—the task was too great. The little boy picked up one starfish and told the old man . . . "it matters to this one," and proceeded to throw it back into the ocean.

The concept of making an impact can be summed up in the words of Nobel Peace Prize winner Elie Wiesel:

But where was I to start?
The world is so vast.
I shall start with the country I know best, my own.
But my country is so very large.
I had better start with my town.
But my town, too, is large.
I had better start with my street.
No, my home.
No, my family.
Never mind.
I shall start with myself.

CHAPTER SIX

ON REACHING THE TOP

C harles Dickens once wrote in the beginning of the *Tale of Two Cities,* "It was the best of times and it was the worst of times." Somehow, that quote seemed to accurately sum up what it is like to reach the top of a personal summit that you have been working towards for over twenty years. At times, I have compared the climb up the ladder of success to climbing a mountain. It was ironic that just before I started on my final ascent up to the "coveted" position of CEO, I had gone to Nepal and had the opportunity to see Mt. Everest. In his memorable book, *Into Thin Air,* author John Krakouer describes the fateful climb of several groups up Mt. Everest in May of 1996. In his book, John describes two altitude related illnesses that sometimes beset climbers, HACE and HAPE (High Altitude Cerebral Edema and High Altitude Pulmonary Edema). The simple version of these illnesses is that as one ascends up the mountain into thinner and thinner air, your brain and arteries begin to turn to Jell-O. Many times, the damage is irreparable or even fatal. As I was now in the very thin air of being a CEO, I began to experience my own altitude sickness. One of the biggest issues that a CEO faces is that you often hang between two worlds, one world is all about the hard stuff, the loans, the financial projections, etc. The other world is all about the soft stuff, people and their families, the excitement of the organization reaching its goals, and the joy and passion around being in the restaurant business. I can remember many nights sitting in the quiet of my office once all of the corporate staff had left. I would sit quietly and think. While I sat and thought, it was as if the weight of the world was right on my shoulders. At times, I felt I was on top of Mt. Everest, the highest point in the world and I could see EVERYTHING. I could see every restaurant, every manager, the families of my employees, the bankers, the lawyers, and everyone else. There were times when I had to leave the office and walk around the block because there just didn't seem to be enough air inside that office for me.

There is a wonderful passage of scripture in Matthew 13 in which Jesus talks about the Parable of the Sower. In its purest sense, Jesus is relating how God's word is sown in the hearts of potential believers and some receive it and some don't receive it. Verse 22 speaks about how the seed is spread among the thorns and the worries of this life and the deceitfulness of wealth chokes the seed and makes it unfruitful. For some reason, this scripture was going over and over in my mind during this time. I had had such noble dreams about what it would be like to be CEO and all of the good that I would do for others. It seemed that the seed that I had planted for me and my company was slowly being choked to death.

I want to be sure that I convey the right impression. As I said in the beginning, "It was the best of times and it was the worst of times." Along with the intense pressure, I experienced some of the most wonderful moments in my entire career up to that point. One such moment was at the General Convention in Nashville, Tennessee in June of 2000. Each year, we would bring all of the restaurant managers and support staff from around the country to celebrate, hand out awards, as well as talk about the goals for the upcoming fiscal year. Usually, I am heavily involved in the preparation of these meetings, but this year, I told my team that it was their full responsibility to pull off this convention. All I planned to do was show up and give my State of the Company Address.

When I arrived in Nashville for the convention, I couldn't have been more impressed. The team had handled all of the details. We had awards, skits, entertainment, and more. I spent the better part of two days laughing along with everyone else, just like a guest. I was so proud of my team. For the first time, they were really running the show and displaying a level of leadership that made me swell with pride and admiration. One of the highlights of the convention was a film that the team put together. The film included highlights from famous movies that would exemplify the five Business Principles that I described earlier:

- ☐ **Dream Big Dreams.**
- ☐ **Play Your Best—Everyday.**
- ☐ **Build Trust With Others.**
- ☐ **Enjoy Yourself Along the Way.**
- ☐ **Make an Impact on the World Around You.**

At the end of this movie, there was a lot of emotion in the convention hall. To my utter surprise, my key team of vice-presidents presented me with an award. The award was a beautiful glass plaque showing each of these five principles with a fun logo that we had developed for each one. As they presented me with this award, they gave me credit for providing the direction and leadership that would allow them to achieve the goals that they had achieved. I will never forget walking up to the stage, accepting the award, and then watching as everyone gave me a standing ovation. When they quieted down, I just stood there for a moment staring at the plaque absolutely speechless. I had watched my team come together over that past several years, and I felt fortunate to be their leader. As I looked at the plaque, I became emotional. I began to speak, but my voice cracked, and all that I could manage was a whisper. With several hundred people still as church mice, I told them that I was indeed at the pinnacle of my career. To be a part of a team like this happens only once in a lifetime. For me, I had just scaled the summit of the highest career mountain that there was. It had been a long and painful journey, but I said that it was all worth it. I also said somewhat prophetically, that if it all ended at that very moment, the journey with all of its struggles would have been worth it just so that I could experience this moment. Little did I realize, God was making plans of His own and would soon call me down from the mountain on to another path.

As I mentioned earlier in this book, I loved the pool when I was growing up. My brother and I, along with "100 of our closest friends," would be at the public pool almost daily during the summer. I remember that my mom had this special whistle that she used to use whenever she wanted my brother and I to come to her. I grew to hate that whistle when I was younger because for me, it was the sound of all of my fun ending for that day. My first response to the whistle was to fake deafness. This worked for a while until all of my friends began to say, "Isn't that your mom calling you?" Busted by my buddies. Usually at the pool, I would hear the whistle a couple of times before my mother would come over to the edge of the pool where I was playing and demand that I get out and get ready to go home. I would get out of the pool and run over to my mother and begin to plead my case to stay. I would usually have purple lips, chattering teeth, and two little hands clasped in front of me like fig leaves. If my first pleading didn't work, I used my last ditch effort of a tantrum. At this point, my mother would simply have all of our things in her arms and would proceed to the car. Having only a pair of swimming trunks to call my own at this point, I was forced to follow my mother to the car, but not without some Academy Award-Winning theatrics as I left. I share that story because it is by far the best description of what happened to me between the convention in Nashville and the day I left the company. During this time, God began to whistle. He began to speak to my heart in only the way He can. At first, I ignored it. I thought, "God must be whistling at someone else. I am the CEO of a $250 million company. I have worked my entire life to get to this point." As far as I was concerned, the "pool" was just starting to feel great. He couldn't. He wouldn't ask me to leave. But God came over to the edge of the pool where I was playing with my friends and said," "It's time to leave, you can't spend your whole life here." As I pulled away from the parking lot of my company, the past twenty years in the restaurant business began to flash in front of me. I saw myself in a fraction of a second go from a polyester-clad assistant manager to a three-piece suit CEO. It seemed like it happened overnight. As I drove away, I knew that I would not return to the restaurant industry because God had something else in store for me.

PART II

PUTTING IT ALL TOGETHER

CHAPTER SEVEN

THE RECOVERING SCOREKEEPER

I was born in 1960. For many of you reading this book, that may sound like ancient history. But 1960 wasn't that long ago. As a young boy in the 60s, my friends and I often played games that reflected the times. My father was in the military, and the United States was at war in Vietnam. It should come as no surprise that the favorite game for my friends and I to play was "Army." The way you played "Army" was to dress up in dark clothes, preferably green or even camouflage for those lucky enough to find some in the attic. We would divide up into teams and each of us would have the requisite weapons, usually toy pistols or rifles. We would proceed to chase each other around the yard and say things like, "I got you, you're dead." "No, I'm not! You missed me by a mile!" Every once and a great while we would sneak up on the "enemy" fortress and capture prisoners. The prisoners were usually the younger brothers and sisters of the enemy who were too little to play but just stayed around the headquarters for fun. At the end of the game, we would count up the number of prisoners. The team with the most prisoners would win.

Being a very driven and competitive young boy, I loved playing Army. I was usually elected captain of our team and would capture the most prisoners. I think that it was at this early age that I began to believe that the key to being happy in life was keeping score and winning. I learned early on that it felt great to win and felt bad to lose. But as I have reflected on my life, I have realized that there is nothing wrong with winning or losing as long as keeping score isn't the main objective.

As I have discussed in Part 1 of this book, my journey of success thus far has been focused a great deal around this topic of keeping score. I remember attending a business management workshop in which many fellow CEOs were present. It was at this time that the speaker coined the phrase "Recovering Scorekeeper." In much the same way that members of Alcoholics Anonymous are referred to as recovering alcoholics, many of us in the room admitted to being recovering scorekeepers. The term means that we live to keep score. We live to win and collect all of the prizes that life has to offer. We shamefully admit that keeping score is very important in our lives. I want to be clear about the fact that I believe that winning and having a winning attitude about life is important. Unfortunately, many of us fall prey to what the popular bumper sticker on a car once read, "Whoever dies with the most toys wins." Jesus said it best in Luke 12:15 when He said that a man's life consists not in the abundance of things which he possesses. If we focus so much on keeping score and winning, we may chase after the wrong goals and dreams in search of things that may not make the best use of all of our God given skills and abilities. Remember, Jesus didn't say that there was anything wrong with having things; however, having things is not the point in life.

As we examine Part 2 of this book, we will explore this issue by focusing on several key areas:

☐ Having a clearly defined personal vision/mission for your life
☐ Unleashing the power of Principle-Centered Goal Setting
☐ Understanding the laws of effective decision-making

CHAPTER EIGHT

WHO ARE YOU AND WHY ARE YOU HERE? UNDERSTANDING YOUR PERSONAL MISSION IN LIFE

**"He who knows others is learned.
He who knows himself is wise."
Lao Tzu**

When I was a new Assistant Manager in the fast food business, I was asked to participate in a "tour." In the fast food business, a tour was when a parade of senior executives would land in a city and proceed to visit one restaurant after another. At each restaurant, we would be inspected for friendliness, speed of service, food quality, and cleanliness. These events were exciting and exhausting all at the same time. I was living in New Orleans at the time, and the tour was to take place in the middle of the summer. To say the least, New Orleans in the summer is hot. New Orleans in the summer in the fast food business is even hotter. It is almost guaranteed that air conditioning will malfunction in the middle of July and work perfectly in the middle of January. I was assigned to one of the highest volume restaurants in the entire region as well as one of the more modern designed locations. All of the managers and employees met at the restaurant and received a laundry list of tasks that needed to be performed prior to the arrival of the senior executives. The list of tasks appeared to me to look something like this:

- ☐ Drain the Gulf of Mexico with a spoon.
- ☐ Detail-clean the Superdome with a toothbrush.
- ☐ Solve world hunger.

Needless to say, the list of tasks to be accomplished looked almost too much to handle. However, we fast food people were a determined group and no job was too difficult.

We spent four long weeks working day and night at the restaurant to prepare it for the inspection. This was in addition to working our normal shifts and taking care of the day to day business. On the day of the tour, I arrived at the restaurant early in the morning. Since it was my day off and I had just closed the night before, I looked a little rough. I was in wrinkled street clothes and had not shaved. As a brand new assistant manager, I thought that I would be praised for rolling out of bed and rushing into the restaurant so quickly that I couldn't even shave. Surely, the senior executives of the company would see such a hard working go-getter as upper management material. As fate would have it, I was in the back of the restaurant doing some final cleaning when two of the local multi-unit managers came to insure that everything was ready and that everyone was looking sharp. When they found me in the back of the restaurant, one of them glared at me and shouted, "Who are you and why are you here?" I was so stunned by the verbal assault that I barely stammered out, "My name is Morgan Hill and I am the Assistant Manager."

Instead of receiving the previously mentioned praise for my dedication, he told me that he didn't care who I was because I was out of uniform and unshaven. To make matters worse, he told me that the car with all of the top senior executives would be at this restaurant any second. With no time to lose, I dashed out the back door and into my car just as the executives pulled into the restaurant. I narrowly missed a disaster and lived to tell about it.

In the end, the tour went well. But the words that were spoken to me over twenty years ago, have stayed with me to this day. Of course, at the time, the multi-unit manager's question was not intended for deep reflection and insight. I caught that the moment he said it. However, as I left the food business as a CEO, I found myself being asked this question again, "Who are you and why are you here?"

As I have examined this question, I have to be honest that I have really struggled. I think that if each of us went under truth serum, we would find that if we were asked this question, we would answer in terms that are all about the roles and responsibilities that we have in life:

- ☐ **I am a business person.**
- ☐ **I am a parent.**
- ☐ **I am involved in community service.**
- ☐ **I am an elected official.**

All of the roles and responsibilities that we have in life are very important, but all too often we use them to define who we are. In my life, I used my titles and my roles to define who I was and what I was supposed to do. From the time I was a young man, I was the captain of the soccer team, the president of the student body and the good son who provided for the household. As I grew up, I was the husband and provider or I was the President and CEO. After the failure of my marriage and retiring from the restaurant business, I found myself in a very awkward position. For the first time in my life, I was simply . . . Morgan Hill . . . human being. This message came home to me when I was at a board of directors meeting for a local charity. Approximately fifteen to twenty business leaders from all over the country were sitting at a large boardroom table. One by one, we were asked to introduce ourselves and say what we did. I was right in the middle of this group. When the introductions began, my mind began to scramble. I was in a room filled with people with titles, and I didn't have one anymore. It reminded me of the dream that I believe many of us have had in which we find ourselves in a public place—completely undressed! In the dream as some of you may recall, we don't know how we came to be in this predicament, but here we are in the middle of the crowd, without a stitch of clothing. Well, I felt very naked at this point. As the introduction process finally came to me, I heard myself say, "My name is Morgan Hill and I work with the foundation." I desperately wanted to let everyone who didn't know me understand that I was once this powerful CEO, but instead, I just let the introductions ripple around the table.

As I began to look through the Bible, I started to notice other leaders who seemed to go through this same sort of struggle. Exodus Chapters 2 and 3 chronicle the early days of

Moses. He grew up with all of the privileges of the royal family of Egypt, yet he felt something burning in his heart because of the struggles of the Hebrews. After killing an Egyptian who was hurting some of his fellow Hebrews, Moses found himself out in the desert—an outcast. Instead of being part of the royal family with all of its position and privilege, Moses found himself tending flocks in the wilderness.

As I have reflected on this portion of the Bible, I can only imagine what Moses must have been thinking. He was in the best position in the world. He was part of the Egyptian royal family. He felt a burden to rescue his people. He was in a great spot to do something great with his life. Now, he was out in the desert and was a virtual "nobody." How could God have missed out on such a great opportunity to use Moses while he was part of the royal family of Egypt? But Moses needed to undergo his own transformation in the desert. This was the time that God allowed Moses to do a lot of soul searching without all of the distractions of position and title. When God finally revealed Himself to Moses in the burning bush in Exodus Chapter 3, Moses' reaction shows that he had a chance to realize that all of his titles and position did not count for much when it came to God's desire to use him to lead the people of Israel out of Egypt. God needed Moses to realize that without Him, he was no one. In fact, in Exodus 3:11, Moses says, "Who am I that I should go to Pharaoh and bring the Israelites out of Egypt?" It's interesting to note that Moses didn't say, "it's about time you came out here to rescue me. I am royalty and it's time for me to go back to Egypt and be the Great Deliverer." Moses began to understand who he was and why he was there. Most importantly, Moses was now in a position to be used by God for His perfect purpose and in His perfect timing.

Personal Mission:
Understanding Who You Are and Why You're Here

Developing a personal mission is not something new that you create. Rather, it is something that you discover within yourself that has been there all along. The questions that are outlined below will aid you in the process of discovering your personal mission. Don't rush it. This process may take days, weeks, or even months. (Remember, Moses was in the desert for forty years.) Once you have completed your personal mission statement and begin to understand who you are and why you are here, commit the statement to paper and review it often. Key questions to ask yourself:

- ❏ What words would I use to describe myself if I couldn't use my titles that I possess or roles that I play?
- ❏ What unique skills and abilities has God given me to be used for His purpose?
- ❏ What single accomplishment am I most proud of so far in my life?
- ❏ What one thing would I like to do most with my life if money were not an obstacle and success was guaranteed?
- ❏ What are the happiest moments in my life so far and why did I choose them?

❑ Make 2 lists. List 1 – What am I passionate about doing? List 2 – What am I good at doing? Compare and contrast these 2 lists.

❑ If you knew that you had just one year left to live, how would you spend that year?

❑ How would I answer the following question, "Who am I and why am I here?"

This is not meant to be a complete list of questions, but it is meant to help you begin the process of understanding and then developing a clear personal mission statement for your life. This is the first key step in moving in the direction that God wants for each of our lives.

CHAPTER NINE

SAILING THROUGH LIFE

**"For I know the plans I have for you," declares the Lord,
"plans to prosper you and not to harm you,
plans to give you hope and a future."
Jeremiah 29:11**

As I have mentioned throughout this book, I spent many of my early years in Virginia Beach, Virginia. If you live in this area of the country, you will most likely spend a lot of time on the water. I was no different. One of the first things that I learned to do after I learned how to swim was to learn how to sail. I remember one day when I was about nine or ten years old, my brother and I got our first sailboat—it was a Sunfish. For those of you reading this book that were not schooled in Sailing 101, the Sunfish is the most basic sailing boat that exists. It's the equivalent of a bike with "training wheels." The boat is maybe 13-14 feet long with one simple sail, one rope to hold on to, one rudder in the back for steering and turning, and one centerboard to keep the boat from drifting.

Our Dad was not only in the Navy, but he also grew up around the water and knew everything that there was to know (at least what a couple of kids needed to know) about sailing. We listened intently to our father as he taught us what to do.

During the early years of sailing, my brother and I learned some basic principles:

☐ You have to **have a plan** as to where you are going or you will drift off course.

This may seem obvious, however even if we were just out on the water for a day of fun, we had a general idea of where we were going.

☐ You have to be **fully prepared** before you set sail.

We always double-checked all of the equipment. We made sure that we had all of the proper safety gear because once we were out on the water and away from the shore, we couldn't go back.

☐ If you want to get from here to there, **it is never in a straight line.**

Sailing somewhere was never in a straight line. If we wanted to get from one place to the other, we learned how to tack. Tacking is a process of picking points in a forward direction and moving in a zigzag pattern in order to catch the proper amount of wind to move ahead. Although we would move back and forth, we never lost sight of our ultimate destination and where we eventually wanted to go.

❏ You always need to **watch** the shifting conditions around you and **adjust accordingly**.

We always had to watch out for changes in the weather and adjust accordingly. I was always amazed at how quickly the weather would change when we lived in Virginia. It could go from sunny to stormy or from a light breeze to a very windy day. Mother Nature seemed to be a bit unpredictable. We knew that we couldn't change the weather, but we could always be ready for the changes that it brought us.

❏ **Know what to do if the boat flips over.**

Learning how to turn the boat back over was a key lesson to learn because all of the other "stuff" just didn't seem to matter if you sank. Our dad showed us a very simple technique. If the boat flipped over, there was a long board that stuck out of the bottom of the boat called the centerboard. The centerboard was the main rudder that would keep the boat from drifting off course when you sailed. If you flipped over, you had to grab the centerboard and lean all of your body weight on it. Slowly, the weight of your body on this centerboard would gradually bring the boat upright. It was interesting to me that the only way to get the boat upright was to lean on the key part of the boat that kept it on course. No other way existed to get the boat right side up on course.

Although I have spent a lot of time discussing the fundamentals of basic sailing, I find that the analogy is very appropriate. Often, we hear the term "sailing through life" and we take it to mean that someone has got everything "easy." However, if we really sail through life, there are some principles that exist that not only help get us to our destination, but they can help get things right if we get off course. These principles and ideas help form the foundation for what I have called <u>Principle-Centered Goal Setting</u>.

Principle-Centered Goal Setting

Principle-Centered Goal Setting is the next step after you have developed a personal mission and an understanding of what you believe God wants you to do with your life. To use the analogy of sailing, your personal mission statement is like deciding where you want to sail your boat. Once you have a clear idea of where you believe that God wants you to go, it's necessary to start the process of Principle-Centered Goal Setting to help get you there. Principle-Centered Goal Setting is made up of three components:

1) The five biblical principles we outlined earlier
2) The five business principles we outlined earlier
3) A specific set of balanced, written goals for you to follow

The five Biblical Principles, mentioned earlier in this book, form the "centerboard" or the main rudder directionally for our Principle-Centered Goal Setting. As we discuss the tactical steps to forming your goals, they should be made with these five principles in mind. Previously in the discussion of sailing, I mentioned that the centerboard is the main rudder that goes right through the center of the boat and keeps the boat from drifting. Perhaps the most important part of charting a course through life is to be sure that God is truly at the "center" of our lives. As in sailing, we may "flip over" on our journey through life. I have discovered that I flip over when I fail to keep God's principles firmly in place. As we discussed before, the only way to get the boat back upright once it is flipped over is to lean all of your weight onto the centerboard. If we draw this analogy to our life, if we flip over, we can only get back upright if we lean on God's principles.

The five business principles serve to act as the rudder at the back of the boat. Periodically on the journey, you will need to turn left or right, since we said that you never sail in a straight line.

These Business and Biblical Principles along with a clear sense of one's personal mission in life, form the foundation for effective goal setting. In my life, I had lots of well-written goals, but they were done without a God inspired personal mission and without a set of principles to guide me when I got off course. This is the reason that Principle-Centered Goal Setting versus ordinary goal setting is so important. Now, the concept of goal setting is a widely discussed topic. However, many individuals still fail to set any direction for their lives. Now, there are certainly examples of people in the world who have accomplished great things without ever having written down a single goal. I believe, however, that written goal setting is a more effective tool in assisting people in reaching a destination that is aligned with their personal mission and principles. The tactical process of setting and achieving goals serves to act as the sail on the sailboat. Without a sail on your sailboat, you won't get very far.

The first key item to understand regarding goal setting is that there are multiple dimensions to consider as key areas of your life. The areas to consider are:

- ❏ **Career**
- ❏ **Financial**
- ❏ **Health**
- ❏ **Family**
- ❏ **Personal growth and development**
- ❏ **Spiritual**
- ❏ **Social**
- ❏ **Business**

I have found that a major challenge in the process of goal setting is gaining an understanding of where to begin. On the following pages are key statements that I have learned from others over the years for each of the eight areas of goal setting. This stage in the process is the personal assessment stage—**Where are you now?** As you read each of these statements, ask yourself these key questions:

1) **Is the statement true or false?**
2) **How would I like to change this area of my life?**

Career

- ❏ I have made satisfactory progress in my career; I am satisfied where I am today.
- ❏ I am in the industry I want and there is a great future for me.

- ☐ I should consider a career change because I am bored and/or maxed out.
- ☐ I have a strong future with my current company and I intend to stay.
- ☐ I have a specific career plan mapped out over the next five to ten years.
- ☐ I have a clear idea of my ultimate, long term career goals. I seriously devote the time and energy to reach those goals.
- ☐ I have thought clearly through the ongoing personal development that I need to reach my career goals and I have an action plan in place (tapes, books, videos, seminars, classes, mentoring relationships) for my own growth.
- ☐ I have relationships with people who can help my career and professional development, and I am utilizing those relationships.
- ☐ I have the formal education/degree that I need to advance right now to the next step in my career.
- ☐ I have identified the skills training that I need to reach my ultimate career goals and I have the plans in place to acquire that training.

Financial

- ☐ I currently live well within my means.
- ☐ I currently save at least 10 percent of my income.
- ☐ I manage my money well and am a good steward of God's resources.

☐ I need the advice of a financial expert and I don't have it.

☐ My family has a family budget and we live within it.

☐ My will or living trust is up to date and accurate.

☐ I pay my credit cards bills each month to stay current.

☐ I know my net worth.

☐ I have a specific long term financial plan.

☐ I earn less than most people my age and it bothers me.

☐ I proudly pay my bills on time.

☐ Money is important to me but I'm satisfied that I keep it in perspective with the other goals in my life.

☐ I am an impulsive spender and it hurts me financially.

☐ My earnings have increased each year for the last five years.

☐ My credit rating is good and problem free.

☐ I have all of the proper medical and life insurance to protect myself and my family.

Health

☐ I rarely miss work due to illness.

☐ I look great physically...I take care of my body and I am healthy.

☐ I have lots of energy and vitality.

☐ I have only healthy stress—the kind associated with exciting challenges.

☐ I have defined goals for physical fitness.

☐ My weight is within my ideal range.

☐ I have regular medical examinations.

☐ I often feel depressed.

☐ I get plenty of rest and sleep well.

☐ I eat a well-balanced low-fat diet.

Family

☐ I get along with my siblings.

☐ I have told my parents that I love them in the last thirty days.

☐ I have a loving, caring marriage or relationship with a significant other.

☐ My spouse (or significant other) and I regularly push each other to grow and develop emotionally and spiritually.

☐ I tell my children how important they are to me and that I love them.

☐ My children tell me they love me and I know that they mean it.

☐ I am a good leader and role model within my family.

☐ I respect that members of my family need time for themselves, to be alone or with others. I am happy for them when they do.

☐ I treat all members of my family the way I like to be treated—with consideration and courtesy.

☐ I live in a home and neighborhood that I love.

Personal Development

- ☐ I follow through on all of my commitments.
- ☐ I am in control of my temper.
- ☐ I recover well from setbacks and disappointments.
- ☐ I am optimistic about myself and my future.
- ☐ I enjoy learning new things.
- ☐ I schedule regular time for new personal development learning such as books, tapes, seminars, workshops, classes, etc.
- ☐ I can be counted on to be on time.
- ☐ I am not afraid of change. I welcome it.
- ☐ Persistence is a problem for me. I seem to bail out at the first sign that things are not going my way.
- ☐ I have trouble believing that I am worthy of the kinds of things that successful people accomplish.
- ☐ I am satisfied with the level of formal education that I have achieved.
- ☐ I stay current in my field, with trends, new products, etc.
- ☐ I am highly self-motivated.
- ☐ I plan my day and week effectively—then I work my plan.

Spiritual .

- ☐ I trust and believe in God.
- ☐ I always tell the truth—no matter what.
- ☐ I have clear personal core values and I live by them.
- ☐ I can be counted on by others.
- ☐ I have strong religious beliefs.

☐ I have a strong sense of purpose and mission for my life. I have a written personal mission statement that I review on a daily/weekly basis.

☐ I make decisions and choose my relationships based on my values.

☐ I try to use sound character and ethical principles when influencing others.

☐ I am always looking for ways to improve my character. I devote scheduled time each week to character building activities.

☐ I believe in taking personal responsibility for my choices and actions.

Social

☐ I have many great friends and I feel blessed in this area of my life.

☐ I am there for people when they need me and vice versa.

☐ I have a best friend or soul mate.

☐ I make people feel great about themselves.

☐ My social calendar is satisfying.

☐ I have self confidence when I am with other people.

☐ I have a good sense of humor.

☐ I am an excellent listener and I listen more than I talk.

☐ I am a people person; I enjoy people and like being around them.

☐ I respect that each person is an individual and I resist the temptation to compare one with the other.

- ☐ I respect the goals, wishes, and dreams of my friends. I provide encouragement for them to succeed.
- ☐ I am comfortable in social situations and do not need to be the center of attention.
- ☐ I do not gossip or talk ill of others when they are not present.
- ☐ I am at ease in social business events and I am sure that others feel it.

Current Business

- ☐ I am respected at work.
- ☐ My work environment is productive and inspiring.
- ☐ My current company gives me fulfillment toward my personal core purpose and mission.
- ☐ My current company shares the same important core values that I have.
- ☐ I am an effective leader of others.
- ☐ I have the technical knowledge and skills to perform my job effectively.
- ☐ My compensation is in line with my performance and contribution.
- ☐ I consistently meet or exceed my goals at work.
- ☐ I handle myself well in business situations and meetings.
- ☐ I get along well with my supervisor, co-workers my customers and suppliers.
- ☐ I am clear and in agreement with my current company's goals and objectives.

The above process, if done correctly, is quite detailed and can be pretty tiring. One of the best suggestions I ever received about goal setting is to set aside a personal one to two day retreat each year to work through it. It is recommended that you go somewhere that will provide you with uninterrupted time to reflect on your journey thus far as well as to realign your direction to insure that it's on course with your personal mission. The investment made in this one day will reap tremendous dividends for your future.

Once you have done the assessment, the next step is to put the information into a series of written goals that you can begin to achieve. Listed below are some suggested guidelines to follow when putting them together:

❏ **All goals should pass the SMART test. They are Specific, Measurable, Attainable, Realistic, and Time-sensitive.**

❏ **All goals should be written down for on-going reference and evaluation.**

❏ **All goals should be organized based on the eight categories that were listed above to insure balance in an individual's life.**

The concept of Principle-Centered Goal Setting and understanding one's own personal mission in life has only one real purpose: **To use all of our God-given talents to the best of our ability to make an impact on the world around us.** Matthew 25:14-30 talks about the parable of the talents. In this parable, there is a very clear point and that is, to use what we have and we will be entrusted with more. In my travels, I meet many people who battle with what I call a "this OR that" mentality. They often see service as either full-time from the pulpit, in the mission field or nothing at all. I fell prey to the same sort of thinking. I failed to realize that God has a "this AND that mentality." He can help us use these business and biblical principles along with our unique giftedness to accomplish great things for others. All of this comes about only through careful planning and hard work. We will get out of life not only what we put into it, but also what we expect out of it. A great poet once wrote these words that helps to illustrate this point:

"I bargained with Life for a penny
And Life would pay no more
However I begged at evening
When I counted my scanty store

For Life is a just employer
He gives you what you ask
But once you have set the wages
Why you must bear the task

I worked for a menial's hire
Only to learn dismayed
That any wage I had asked of Life
Life would have willingly paid."

Whatever we ask for from life, that we <u>believe in</u> and are willing to <u>work hard for</u>, we CAN receive. However, we must combine the principles outlined here with our natural talents to become a person who truly makes a difference. Success in all of the eight dimensions requires on-going evaluation and improvement. A commitment to building and improving all of the areas of one's life, versus only one or two areas is a key step in making the most of your life.

CHAPTER TEN

"DECISIONS . . . DECISIONS . . . DECISIONS"

One of my favorite movies is *Indiana Jones and the Last Crusade*. I am sure that many of you reading this book have seen this movie at least once or twice. As the story goes, Indiana Jones and his father are off on another adventure. In this case, the two are in a race with Nazi Germany to find the Holy Grail, believed to be the cup that Jesus drank from at the Last Supper. In the movie, each of the good guys believes that the cup is sacred and holy. The bad guys only want the cup because they think it will bring them power and immortality. In the final scene of the movie, the bad guys and Indiana Jones both get to the Holy Grail at the same time. The only problem is that there are many cups to choose from, and they are in all shapes and sizes. The old knight that has been guarding the Holy Grail gives these very wise words to both parties, "Choose wisely, for just as the cup of Christ will bring you life, the other cups will bring you death." The bad guys picked a cup that was beautiful to look at and appeared on the outside to be the right one, but it was a fake. As expected, the person who drank from this cup died. Indiana Jones looked over all of the other cups and then saw a very plain piece of pottery that most anyone would have overlooked. Once Indiana Jones drank from the cup and was alright, the knight said to Indiana, "You have chosen wisely."

I love this story because it points out so clearly that life is a series of decisions, decisions, and more decisions. Decisions that may look good on the outside may not prove to be the best courses of action. Experience has taught me that there are several key laws about decision-making. Some of these may be new to you and others may sound familiar. I like to call them:

1.   **The Law of the Big Rocks**
2.   **The Law of the Farm**
3.   **The Law of Affection**

Law #1 – The Law of Big Rocks

" The tougher the choices we make early in life, the more choices we will have later in life."

Matthew 7:13-14 lays out a clear formula for decision making. It says:

"Enter through the narrow gate. For wide is the gate and broad is the way that leads to destruction, and many enter through it. But small is the gate and narrow the road that leads to life, and only a few find it."

Following this formula often means not only doing the tough stuff first, but doing the tough stuff often. I have attended various seminars that explain the following principle that I like to call the Law of the Big Rocks. As the story goes, there is a person who has a large jar and several stacks of rocks. The first stack of rocks is very heavy and difficult to lift. The second stack of rocks would fit in the palm of your hand. The third stack of rocks is merely pebbles. And finally, there is a pile of sand. The person's task is to fit all of these items into the jar. Usually, the person fills the jar with sand first, then the pebbles, then the medium sized rocks then finally the big rocks. Much to the person's frustration, the jar is full after only getting part of the medium-sized rocks into the jar. At first, he thinks that the jar is the wrong size but he is told that the only way to fit **everything** into the jar is to put the big rocks in **first**.

In life, we love to put the sand and pebbles in first because that is the easy path that is often encouraged by those around us. However, we need to keep in mind that often the best decisions are the toughest. They involve going down the narrow path versus the eight lane interstate. Decision making often means putting the big rocks of life in the jar first. These big rocks are often issues such as:

- ☐ **Living by biblical principles vs. worldly principles**
- ☐ **Balancing time between family and career**
- ☐ **Pursuing lifelong personal growth and education**
- ☐ **Giving of your time in service to others within the community**

These big rocks are hard to put in the jar; however, putting them in early in life will often bear much more fruit for us later in life.

The Law of the Farm – "We reap what we sow"

When I was growing up in Virginia, my father, brother and I would often go bird hunting in the fall. We would get all of our gear packed up and travel out to some neighboring farms in order to hunt. I was always impressed with farmers because they were the hardest working people I had ever met. They were always doing something. They were planting various crops, they were working on the equipment, they were harvesting crops for sale at the local market, they just never quit. During this time, I learned an important principle for life without ever realizing it. <u>We reap what we sow</u>. As I would sit out in the fields waiting for the birds to fly overhead, I would see the farmers harvesting crops in the fields next to me. There was never a time that I didn't see them working. There was also never a time in which they harvested corn out of a field where they had planted cotton. Or if they planted barley, they didn't get soybeans. I know that this sounds like such a basic principle, but somehow in our lives, we miss this key in the Law of Decision-Making. We can't sow one thing and reap another. It violates all of the laws of nature. We can't sow deceit and reap honesty. We can't sow laziness and reap financial rewards. We can't sow neglect of family and friends and reap healthy relationships. Galatians 6:7-9 says it best:

> **Do not be deceived: God is not mocked. A man reaps what he sows. The one who sows to please his sinful nature, from that nature will reap destruction. The one who sows to please the Spirit, from the Spirit will reap**

eternal life. Let us not become weary in doing good, for at the proper time, we will reap a harvest if we do not give up.

The Law of Affection

I am a big animal lover. Specifically, I love dogs. (I don't dislike cats, but I love dogs.) Over the last ten years, I have been blessed not only to have several small dogs, but I have also had the opportunity to serve my community by helping with the local humane society. A few years ago, we rescued a family of schnauzer puppies, and we were tasked with raising them before they were adopted out to various families. As these puppies began to grow, they loved to play with their little toys. One toy in particular was a simple red rubber ball. I would sit on the floor with these three puppies and throw this ball to them for what seemed to be hours. When one of them would grab the ball and bring it back, I would then hold the ball out in front of them just before I would throw it again. I can vividly remember six little eyes that were fixated on this red ball. If I moved the ball to the right, their little eyes would go to the right. If I moved the ball to the left, their little eyes would go to the left. I imagined the only thing going through their little minds at that moment was, "Red ball, red ball, pleeeeeease throw the red ball!" They absolutely loved it. I was able to influence their direction because I had in my hand the object of their affection.

In our lives, the Law of Affection has a tendency to influence more of our decisions than almost anything else. We can all remember a time when we went somewhere or did something when we thought we were in love, that didn't turn out the way we planned. Or perhaps we can recall a time when we had a passion to fulfill a dream that guided us in the right direction. I believe that Jesus offers us a wonderful role model for this Law of Affection.

If we take a look at the life of Jesus, He spent approximately thirty years preparing for the work that He was meant to perform while He was here on earth. He definitely knew who He was and why He was here. His Personal Mission Statement might best be summed up in these words: "To give up His life as a ransom for many." In addition to having a clear sense of purpose based on His love for His Father in heaven as well as His love for mankind, He had two very clear goals that can be seen in the New Testament:

1) **To fulfill God's prophesies and get to the cross**
2) **To pour His life into twelve men who would change the world for generations**

Even though Jesus had a clear sense of direction based on His affection, He was faced with temptations to deviate from His course. The Gospel of Matthew talks about the temptation of Christ. I have read this passage from the Bible many times, but it struck me recently that Jesus really did have a choice early in His ministry to stay on course or to deviate. For many years, I simply glossed over this passage with the assumption that Jesus **couldn't** give in to temptation, but as I have read more of the Bible, I learned that **He wouldn't give in to temptation**.

When presented with the easy path to fame and glory by Satan, He stayed the course based on His affection for all of mankind. He knew that this right decision would reap a harvest for eternity.

I will conclude this book the way I started. I never imagined that I would ever write a book of any kind. However, this book is just my reflection of how God can be merciful enough to love us redirect us to fulfill His purposes. As you have seen, I was way off course. I had not remembered to keep God at the center, and as a result, my life "flipped over." But God has been kind enough to teach me some very valuable lessons that have allowed me to lean on His principles and get my life moving back in the direction that He wants me to go.

Currently, I get the opportunity to work with three groups of people. I work with college students, CEO's and business leaders, and senior adults. It's interesting that with college students the issue is often one of "confusion." They have so much of their life ahead of them that they often don't know exactly which path to take. With CEO's and business leaders the issue is often "frustration." A couple of decades has gone by since college, and the dreams aren't going according to "plan." Finally, with senior adults the issue is one of "desperation." They are now in the twilight of their lives. Many seniors I visit with wonder how the time has flown by so quickly and how they could have lived their lives differently. As I look at the world around me, many times talking with people that are sixty years apart, I have come to the definite conclusion that God is not random, and we are all here for a reason. He has a plan for each our lives. He wants each of us to use all of our talents and gifts to change the world around us. However, we must be willing to take the necessary steps to uncover His purpose for our life and then take the tough steps to turn that purpose into reality. Along the way, we will be faced with a lot of tough choices. It is my hope and prayer that the thoughts and ideas outlined in this book will help you with some of those tough choices and guide you as you become all that God intended you to be.

REFERENCES

This book is a combination of my personal experiences, timely literature on the subject, as well as the insights from other business professionals. I would like to thank and acknowledge them here:

Rick Houcek – Soaring with Eagles Inc.
>   Seminar on Effective Goal Setting

Viktor E. Frankl
>   *Man's Search for Meaning*
>   Washington Square Press/1959

RTM Restaurant Group/Winners International Inc.
>   TRUST Model for Effective Team Interaction
>   5 Business Principles for Long Range Planning

Author Contact Information

Morgan Hill Consulting Inc.
2295 Towne Lake Parkway Suite #116-234
Woodstock, GA 30189

email: morganhill1@msn.com

Printed in the United States
5318